The Keswick to Borrowdale Bus

Stuart Emmett

I hope you enjoy the journey through this book which has been very pleasurable to research and write and could not have happened without the many wonderful photographers who recorded history for us. Thanks are especially due to John Bennett, who was of exceptional assistance.

My royalties from the book sales, after deduction of production costs, are going 100% to assist on bus preservation/archives and some of the image providers have supplied their photos free of charge to help this worthy initiative.

Text © Stuart Emmett, 2020.
First published in the United Kingdom, 2020,
reprinted 2023, 2024, 2025,
by Stenlake Publishing Ltd.,
54-58 Mill Square,
Catrine, Ayrshire,
KA5 6RD

Telephone: 01290 551122
www.stenlake.co.uk

Printed by P2D, 1 Newlands Road, Westoning, MK45 5LD

ISBN 9781840338850

**The publishers regret that they cannot supply
copies of any pictures featured in this book.**

Picture Acknowledgements

Where no name is stated, the pictures are from my own collection that is made up of our family pictures and other sources. For the latter, where the original photographer cannot be traced, I offer my apologies to them for the lack of accreditation and would be pleased to correct this in any future edition.

The Bus Archive; includes pictures from J.R. Wingfield, C.F. Klapper, D.S. Giles, and Roy Marshall: pages 12, 14, 15, 23, 28 (lower), 29 (lower), 30 (lower), 31 (both), 32 (both), 34, 36, 37 (upper), 50, 53.
J.S.Cockshott, The Transport Library: pages 3, 6 (lower), 11, 37 (lower).
Geoffrey Morant, The Transport Library: page 43.
PM Photography: pages 10, 54.

The Bus Gallery: pages 46, 48, 51, 55.
R.C. Davies: pages 30 (upper), 33 (upper).
Geoff Lumb, Travel Lens Photographic: page 29 (upper).
John Bennett: pages 45, 52.
U.K. Classic Bus Photos: page 42.
K.D. Jubb: pages 35, 40 (both).

References

Commercial Motor, 24th August 1951, 7th March 1958, 13th November 1959, 22nd August 1969
The PSV Circle. *Cumberland Motor Services*, ref 2PA11, October 2013
Harry Postlewaite, *Cumberland Motor Services 1912 to 2012*, Venture Publications, 2012

It all began in 1954

As a youngster, in 1954 we went camping for our annual holiday to Seatoller in Borrowdale; around 8 miles from Keswick. At Keswick we caught the Borrowdale bus, which has been advertised as "the most spectacular route in England".

To get to Keswick from our home in Bradford, we used the X87 summer only service, operated by the splendidly named, West Yorkshire Road Car Company and run jointly with Ribble Motor Services. It could be a busy route, especially during the two weeks annual holiday periods in West Yorkshire. There were regular duplicates on the X87 in the peak summer season with often hired-in coaches from small independents.

Ribble 214. at Bradford Chester Street Station on 16th August 1958 is a duplicate on the X87. Looks like people are waiting to get access, but it would be a "hard" ride on this service bus for the five hours to Keswick (maybe though, it was a short to Kendal or Ambleside?). 214 was in a series of 27 (201 to 227) re-bodied 1935/1936 Leyland TS7s with chassis from Devon General (like 214), Yorkshire Woollen and Ribble that in 1949 had received new Burlingham B35F bodies.

The X87 ran from Leeds via Bradford up the A65, and from Skipton this road was also the "main line" for the Pennine Motor Services black, cream, and orange Leylands. They ran to Gargrave (with a branch route off to Malham), and also to Settle, Ingleton, Lancaster and Morecambe. Skipton was an interesting place for buses; another book in this series covers Skipton and the Pennine, Laycock, Ribble and West Yorkshire buses.

After Skipton, the X87 would stop for a short break, between Settle and Ingleton, at the former Cross Streets Hotel at Austwick. This was a scheduled stop for the X87 and also for the X88 from Leeds to Morecambe. In summer peak times there were twelve such scheduled refreshment stops for the X87/88, starting at 1011 hours with an X88 to Morecambe and finishing at 2026 hours with two buses on the X88, one bound for Leeds and one for Morecambe (the drivers crossed over buses at Cross Streets so they could return to their home depot).

Returning from Keswick in August 1954, the LS5G dual purpose West Yorkshire EUG18 on the left had only entered service a month earlier, and the coach LS6G number CUG2 was from June 1952. Both were for Bradford, and perhaps the buses behind, including what looks like a Ribble Leyland integral Olympic with Weymann B44F body, were running on to Leeds.

The journey from Cross Streets continued on the A65 passing through Settle, Ingleton and Kirby Lonsdale, arriving in the Lake District at Kendal and then on to Windermere, Ambleside, and Grasmere. From Kendal it was always a busy road with coaches and the local Ribble stage services, especially the legendary 555 from Lancaster to Keswick, gave added variety.

Running through Ambleside to the bus station in the early 1950s you passed by a Brown's Luxury Coaches bus for Hawkshead and Sawry Ferry Landing. Brown's used two Commer Commandos of which JM7316 is loading. Both had Barnaby of Hull bodies and worked until 1960 when they were replaced by a 1951 Mulliner military style bodied Bedford SB LXJ318 that had been new to Mayne in Manchester. It lasted only two years. In June 1962 the service was sold to Ribble who then used the bus station down the road on the left.

Left: *Brown's other Commer JM8303 in a Barnaby bodybuilders shot.*

Below: *Ambleside Bus Station in 1951. The Leyland TD Alexander double deckers have been on route 555 and the Leyland TS single deckers all show route 517 that went to Barrow but with opportunity for many short workings such as to nearby Windermere. The bus on the far right was another TS7 in the 201-227 series; this one had a chassis from Yorkshire Woollen.*

Ambleside Bus Station. The depot, whose roof is visible on the left side, was accessed from the adjoining road. An all Leyland coach is leaving and on the stands is an all Leyland double decker with rear doors and a Leyland/Weymann integral Olympic. The X87 would pull in to unload on its way to Keswick.

After Ambleside and Grasmere the hill up Dunmail Raise slowed down our Bristol LS on the climb, then down into the valley again past Thirlmere, a natural lake enlarged to form a reservoir in the 19th century for Manchester Corporation who constructed a dam at the northern end to provide that city with water supplies via the 96 mile-long mainly gravity feed aqueduct. Helvellyn Ridge is to the east of Thirlmere.

Just out of Keswick on the Penrith road with the snow-covered Blencathra in the background, Cumberland KRM265 is on the joint 74 service with Ribble. An all Leyland PD2/12 from 1951 and the penultimate batch for Cumberland, as then Bristol/ECW buses became mandatory. Ribble and Cumberland stage buses, at the time, only met in Carlisle, Keswick/Penrith, and Millom.

Keswick was soon reached and in 1954 was a much quieter place compared to the Ambleside/Windermere area. There was no nearby M6 and no dual carriageway roads. However, there was a railway branch line between Keswick and Workington with around ten journeys per day. Since 1954 car traffic has increased exponentially, the railway has closed and part of the track taken for the A66 that runs between and Workington and Penrith and gives access to the M6. Keswick is now a busy tourist area, rivalling the Ambleside/Windermere area.

The X87 was scheduled to arrive in Keswick at 1311 hours parked up before loading and returning at 1446 hours. Buses entered Keswick Bus Station from the left. The X87 stopped next to where the Ribble all Leyland on the 74 to Penrith is in the photo. The exit was then to turn left, past the Ribble all Leyland coach and then left again, past the top of a Cumberland bus that can just be seen above the coach. The single level building had toilets, a café, and offices. The white building behind is the Cumberland bus depot. The coach parking area was exceptionally large. On the right parked up are two Cumberland double deckers, a Bristol LD and a Leyland PD2. Next to them are excursion coaches. Some of the stage buses that could be seen in Keswick are shown on the following pages.

Cumberland 1948 Bedford OB 251 is resting at Keswick Bus Station and followed the CMS pre-war practice to paint lightweight coaches in the bus livery. Had it been on a Borrowdale run, or on some other service? Most of the six Cumberland OBs were loaned to West Yorkshire for the summer seasons in 1949 and 1951. Behind to the left is a CMS Leyland PD2, with another Ribble PD2 to the right.

On 22nd June 1964 is the soon to be withdrawn Ribble all Leyland PD2 1950 DRN242 loading for Penrith, a 65-minute journey. It has rear doors, useful for the exposed road to Penrith.

Keswick is the end of the iconic 555 route from Lancaster. In 1954 Route 68 ran from Keswick to Lancaster, took three hours and five minutes and ran hourly. The 555 ran hourly from Kendal to Keswick, a one-hour 53-minute journey. This gave a 30-minute headway between Kendal and Keswick. Above is LRN63, a Leyland PD3/3 with Burlingham H72F body new to Scout in May 1958 and with the Ribble take-over of Scout it became S22, until l968, when it became Ribble 1975. The bus is unusual in not having its Leyland original middle radiator panel as this has been replaced by one from Ribble's fleet of full fronted PD3s. The view dates from sometime after 1968 by which time the 555 went all the way to Lancaster.

Cumberland ORM137 was the first double decker batch of Bristol/ECW buses in 1955. Seen here in December 1961 with fleet number 402, it had rear doors and in 1959 had been fitted with high backed seats (often known as country seats) for use on longer services. It would have run into Keswick from Whitehaven on the 34/35 routes taking just under two hours, (from Embleton, the 34 went to the west of side of Bassenthwaite Lake and the 35 to the east side). At Keswick, 402 then worked the 37, a 15-minute short on route 34 to Thornthwaite.

The Borrowdale bus

Once at Keswick, we walked up the main street from the bus station to Moot Hall in the Market Square to catch the bus up to Seatoller.

Askew's Bedford OB GRM914 has just arrived from Seatoller without a side radiator cover. On the left, just past the row of cars behind GRM914, is the Moot Hall/Market Square that was used for Borrowdale departures.

Ready for Seatoller in Borrowdale is Simpson's Commer HRM108. The Moot Hall just appears to the right above what looks like a Jowett Bradford van.

Once at Moot Hall we loaded the rucksacks into the boot of the bus and off we went up the Borrowdale Valley. Even then it was a tourist location, with hotels, guesthouses, B&Bs, youth hostels and camp sites and catered for the lowland visitor as well as the hill walker who was able to choose from a range of mountains, including England's highest, Scafell Pike (which is correctly pronounced as in the original spelling of Scawfell, and not, as Scarfell).

This Borrowdale bus of Young's is the long-serving HRM48 from 1948 and is seen at the Market Square in Keswick in July 1964. The passageway to the right is Pack House Court which led to the office of Weightmans on the right, and on the left Papes Garages, Motors and Tours Limited. The following guide shows this.

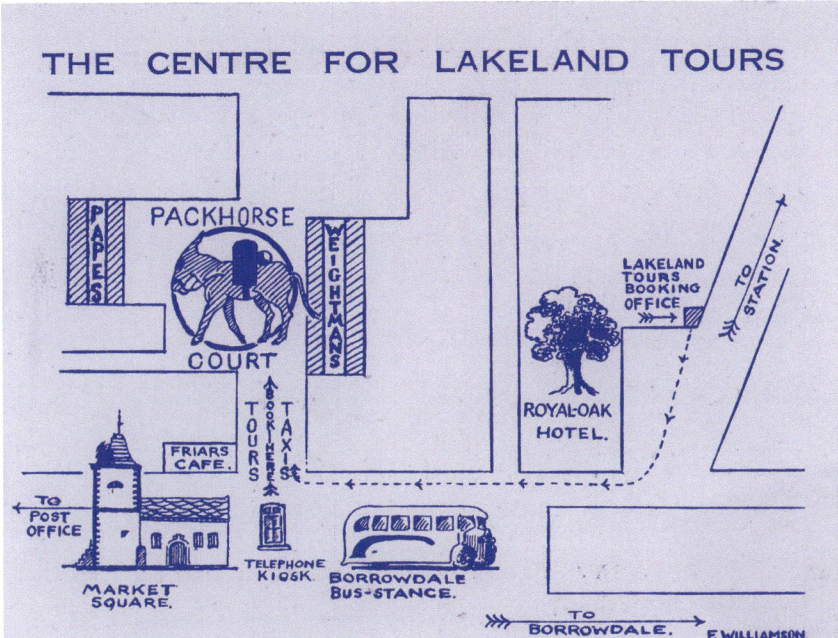

The bus journey from Keswick up to Borrowdale, also known as "the most beautiful bus ride in England," is just less than 8 miles and passes through some delightful and flat river valley countryside; indeed, the height difference between Keswick and Seatoller is less than 50 feet. The first mile took us out of Keswick between the fields, until we could see Derwentwater lake on the right side with Castlerigg Fell rising steeply on the left. After ten minutes from Keswick we came to the Lodore Falls and the Lodore Hotel. After this, we left the lake behind and at 15 minutes out of Keswick, we were at the halfway point at Grange in Borrowdale. Here was based, W.L. Askew. one of the five operators of the route in 1954.

Right: *A 1934/1935 timetable of Askew's. At this time, each operator published their own timetable.*

Schedule 2.   1934—35.

ASKEW'S
BORROWDALE SERVICE
RUNS DAILY BETWEEN
KESWICK AND SEATOLLER,
Leaving TOP MARKET SQUARE, KESWICK.

Leaves	a.m.	a.m.	*p.m.	p.m.	p.m.	p.m.	p.m.	S p.m.	Fares.	
									single	return
KESWICK	9-15	10-35	12-0	1-5	2-15	3-45	5-50	7-0		
DEER CLOSE	9-19	10-39	12-4	1-9	2-19	3-49	5-54	7-4	2d.	4d.
BARROW HOUSE	9-22	10-42	12-7	1-11	2-22	3-52	5-57	7-7	4d.	6d.
LODORE HOTEL	9-25	10-45	12-10	1-14	2-25	3-55	6-0	7-10	6d.	10d.
Borro'dale hotel	9-28	10-48	12-13	1-16	2-28	3-58	6-3	7-13	7d.	1/-
GRANGE	9-30	10-50	12-15	1-18	2-30	4-0	6-5	7-15	9d.	1/2
BOWDER STONE	9-33	10-53	12-18	1-21	2-33	4-3	6-8	7-18	11d.	1/3
ROSTHWAITE	9-36	10-57	12-22	1-25	2-37	4-7	6-12	7-22	1/1	1/6
Stonethwaite Rd	9-38	11-1	12-26	1-27	2-41	4-11	6-16	7-26	1/2	1/7
SEATOLLER arrive	9-42	11-5	12-30	1-30	2-45	4-15	6-20	7-30	1/3	1/9

Leaves	a.m.	*a.m.	*p.m.	p.m.	p.m.	p.m.	S p.m.
SEATOLLER	9-45	11-15	12-30	1-35	3-10	5-15	6-25
Stone'waite (Rd.)	9-49	11-19	12-34	1-39	3-14	5-19	6-29
ROSTHWAITE	9-53	11-23	12-38	1-43	3-18	5-23	6-33
BOWDER STONE	9-57	11-27	12-42	1-47	3-22	5-27	6-37
GRANGE	10-0	11-30	12-45	1-50	3-25	5-30	6-40
Borrowdale Hotel	10-2	11-32	12-47	1-52	3-27	5-32	6-42
LODORE HOTEL	10-5	11-35	12-50	1-55	3-30	5-35	6-45
BARROW HOUSE	10-8	11-38	12-53	1-58	3-33	5-38	6-48
DEER CLOSE	10-11	11-42	12-57	2-2	3-37	5-42	6-52
KESWICK arrive	10-15	11-45	1-0	2-5	3-40	5-45	6-55

SUNDAY SERVICE, April 15th to Sept. 30th.
SUMMER SERVICE, April 15th to Oct. 31st.   WINTER SERVICE, Saturdays Only.
S. Summer Service only.   * Not run on Sundays.

We did not enter the village, which we could see on the right hand side across the bridge over the River Derwent but carried straight on, into a relatively narrow gorge by the Bowder Stone, a 2,000 tonne boulder precariously balanced on one narrow corner.

After the journey from Grange, we appeared out into the valley again, and 25 minutes from Keswick, we passed, or more aptly squeezed, through the small village of Rosthwaite.

Next, we were at a junction where a small road runs off for half a mile into the hamlet of Stonewaite, from where a footpath enters the Langstrath Valley that climbs up into the mountains.

Young's "Red & White" 1935 timetable.

Phone 171. **YOUNG'S** (Original)

RED AND WHITE

BORROWDALE SERVICE

RUNS DAILY BETWEEN

KESWICK AND SEATOLLER,

(UNTIL 30th SEPTEMBER, SUNDAYS INCLUDED),

Leaving TOP MARKET SQUARE, KESWICK.

Leaves	a.m.	a.m.	p.m.	p.m.	p.m.	p.m.	Fares.	
KESWICK	9-45	11-5	1-30	2-55	5-0	6-45	single	return
Ashness Gate	9-50	11-10	1-35	3-0	5-5	6-50	4d.	6d.
Lodore (Falls)	9-55	11-15	1-40	3-5	5-10	6-55	6d.	10d.
Grange	10-0	11-20	1-45	3-10	5-15	7-0	9d.	1/2
Bowder Stone	10-5	11-25	1-50	3-15	5-20	7-5	11d.	1/3
Rosthwaite	10-10	11-30	1-55	3-20	5-25	7-10	1/1	1/6
Stonethwaite Rd	10-12	11-32	1-57	3-22	5-27	7-12	1/2	1/7
Seatoller arrive	10-15	11-35	2-0	3-25	5-30	7-15	1/3	1/9

Leaves	a.m.	a.m.	a.m.	p.m.	p.m.	p.m.	p.m.
SEATOLLER	...	10-30	11-45	2-0	4-0	5-50	7-30
Stone'waite (Rd.)	...	10-33	11-48	2-3	4-3	5-53	7-33
Rosthwaite	...	10-35	11-50	2-5	4-5	5-55	7-35
Bowder Stone	...	10-40	11-55	2-10	4-10	6-0	7-40
Grange	...	10-45	12-0	2-15	4-15	6-5	7-45
Lodore (Falls)	...	10-50	12-5	2-20	4-20	6-10	7-50
Ashness Gate	...	10-55	12-10	2-25	4-25	6-15	7-55
Keswick arrive	...	11-0	12-15	2-30	4-30	6-20	8-0

Office:—81, MAIN STREET, KESWICK.

23 AUG 1935

After Rosthwaite and just before entering the hamlet of Seatoller, another small road goes off the left for a mile down to Seathwaite, which is the wettest inhabited place in England. From Seathwaite a footpath climbs up towards the mountains and to the Sty Head "crossroads" for Scafell Pike, Great Gable, and others, with a view down to Wastwater – Wastwater being pronounced as 'Wast-water' and not 'Waz-water' or 'Wastewater' – and beyond to the Irish Sea.

So after a journey of 30 minutes, we entered and unloaded at Seatoller, after which, the bus reversed ready for the return trip.

Simpson's Commer HRM108 unloading at Seatoller in August 1954, after which it would return to Keswick. Once it had disgorged its load it proceeded through the hamlet and then reversed into an opening to turn round.

The Borrowdale bus service was a shared route with five companies, who in 1954 used the following vehicles:

Operator	Reg. No.	Chassis	Body	Notes
W.L. Askew, Derwent House Hotel and Fern Nursery, Grange in Borrowdale.	GRM914	Bedford OB	SMT C29F	New in 01/48 and bought 06/53 from Mandale in Greystoke, Cumbria.
R.W. Simpson, Victoria Garage, Keswick.	HRM108	Commer Commando	Myers & Bowman B29F	New in 09/48.
Weightman's (Keswick), Ltd., Pack Horse Court, Main Street, Keswick.	HAO950	Commer Q4	Myers & Bowman B29F	New in 07/48 and rebuilt from a wartime lorry chassis.
T. Young & Sons, 81 Main Street and Victoria Street, Keswick.	HRM48	Bedford OB	Duple C29F	New in 09/48.
Cumberland Motor Services, Whitehaven (with a small depot in Keswick).	Varied	Leyland PS1 and others	Varied	See later for more details on the CMS buses.

The two Commers with bodies were from Myers and Bowman, the Commer agents from nearby Distington. They built around 40 buses between 1946 and 1951. Still in business today running a Toyota car dealership near to the Lillyhall Industrial Estate, the place where the 1970s Leyland National plant used to be.

We got to know one of the Borrowdale bus drivers, Mr. Simpson. For this small boy, being able to sit at the front near to "Matey" was always exciting. Indeed, I was hooked on buses from then on and also to the Lake District (and have now retired there).

I was used to seeing bus drivers with a uniform, but in Borrowdale, Mr. Simpson wore a normal shirt, tie, jacket and trousers, with the obligatory flat cap, (although I recall Weightman's driver had a long brown dustcoat and a peaked cap). Sometimes there could be a conductor, but this was rare; therefore, the one-man operation equipment was a cash bag hung over the back of the driver's seat and a handful of tickets (for those that wanted them).

It was always fun travelling on the Borrowdale bus, even when it was full and packed with people standing; loadings were often far in excess of the normal standing rules. In the late afternoon it was usually difficult to get on, especially when trying to do so beyond each terminus. As has been noted by another traveller: "The OBs couldn't expand to infinity! I recall waiting for the bus near Lodore, one summer evening after a long day's hike. I guess there were a dozen or so waiting. Mr Weightman's bus hove into view and everyone stood up expectantly. With a regretful wave from the driver, the bus sailed past – with an apparently solid mass of humanity inside!"

Above: *Inside Simpson's Commer in 1954.*

There were never any duplicates, as three of the operators at the time only had the one bus, and whilst Weightman had a Commer Avenger coach, I never saw it on the route. The 29 seaters were not adequate in the summer peak; however, it was different in winter when, just Simpson and Weightman each worked on alternative weeks.

Weightman's 1950 Commer Avenger coach with Myers & Bowman body that could have been used on the Seatoller route.
Inset: Simpson's 1939 Timetable.

Route History

The PSV Circle suggests Weightman was the first operator in June 1920. Askew had their first vehicle in April 1921 and their service started in 1923, followed on by Simpson in April 1927 and Cumberland MS took the opportunity to run on the route in 1928. Young's came along in 1931 having been reported to have started in Aspatria; they also had a small haulage business in Keswick.

There also seems to have been some involvement on the route from 1921 by Papes Garages Coaches & Motors Ltd of Keswick, who claimed to have run the original four-in-hands horse carriages over the local passes. Papes eventually got into coach excursion work but seem to have ceased on the Seatoller route by 1932. Weightman were reported (*Commercial Motor* 24th August 1951) to have an "associated house of Papes with two Commer 29-seaters" and both originally shared premises on Pack Horse Court. It seems likely that Weightman obtained the former Papes excursions and tours licences as Papes' fleet of three Bedford coaches were by December 1942 with Lewthwaite Brothers in Cleator working on miners' transport. Lewthwaite then was bought by CMS in March 1943. However, further research is needed on this operator.

Papes' four horse and carriage touting for business along with a Bedford WTB open-top coach BRM140 or 159.

Mr William Leyland Askew from Derwent House in Grange-in-Borrowdale was granted a licence in 1931 following the Road Traffic Act. This covered one vehicle for April to October only and the business was run in conjunction with a private hotel. As the only operator in Borrowdale, they also got a licence for excursions from Newlands, the next valley to the west on the road to Buttermere. This seems to have been little used and although it was still held until at least 1964, it was finally surrendered in 1967.

The stage licence that was granted to Askew in 1931 was part of a coordinated summer service between Askew, Cumberland, Simpson, Weightman and Young's, with the winter service being operated by Simpson and Weightman only.

During the Second World War and with fuel rationing, Cumberland withdrew for some years and thus furthered their independence from the other operators as shown by their non-acceptance of return tickets. They also had their own timetables. CMS were not unique in issuing their own timetable; indeed, it was said the only combined timetable that existed was in the chemist shop window in the Market Place.

Wartime brought a reduced service with fifteen daily services in the summer and six in the winter and on a Sunday eight and four departures, respectively. With the Army quartered in Borrowdale, Saturday nights were busy, and Weightman's 26 and 20 seat Commers were once seen carrying more than 70 people.

By 1949 the summer service had a properly combined timetable with, in summer 23 departures daily and ten on a Sunday; for comparison, the 1960 and 1961 timetables had 23 journeys a day in summer, with thirteen on Sundays, this falling in October to twelve and ten before the "full" winter journeys of seven and four journeys, respectively.

The summer 1954 summer timetable and the operators share/allocation is shown on page 70 of Harry Postlethwaite's 2012 book *Cumberland Motor Services 1912 to 2012*. Each fifth day one bus was taken off the route, so there were only four operators on any day. The headway varied from 20 to 45 minutes with the journey taking 30 minutes, and up to a 10-minute layover in Seatoller. The layovers were longer in Keswick and it could mean over an hour's wait until the next turn.

Left: *The composite 1953 timetable.*

In winter Simpson and Weightmans' were still the only operators, each operating the route for one week and then swapping over. This caused some concern at a Traffic Commissioners hearing in February 1958; the following extracts from *Commercial Motor* dated 7th March 1958, tells the full story:

> **Strange Principles in Bus Service**
>
> A bus service between a Lakeland valley and the nearest town was criticized last week by Mr. J. A. T. Hanlon, chairman of the Northern Traffic Commissioners, for its "old fashioned and strange principles." He had been told that five concerns operated between Keswick and Seatoller during the summer season, whilst in winter two concerns operated the route on alternate weeks.
>
> The two winter operators, Messrs. Weightman's, Keswick, and Mr. R. W. Simpson, Keswick, were applying to amend the service. There were objections from Cockermouth Rural District Council, Keswick Urban District Council and Borrowdale Parish Council. The application was adjourned until the summer.
>
> It was stated that the summer service was shared between the applicants and Mr. T. Young, Keswick, Mr. Askew, Grange-in-Borrowdale, and Cumberland Motor Services Ltd. Weightman's and Mr. Simpson wanted to make the 8.25 a.m. Keswick-Seatoller-Keswick run an hour later, to amend the 5.30 p.m. service to 5.50 p.m., and to suspend the 6.45 p.m. service on the ground that it was unremunerative.
>
> It had been suggested that a new company should be formed to hold the licences, with all the operators sharing, but so far this had come to nothing.
>
> Mr. W. Hind, clerk to the parish council, told the Commissioners that operators did not duplicate buses in summer because some of them had only one vehicle. Each fifth day one bus was taken off the route, so there were then only four operators. He suggested that each operator should run the winter service in turn for one week.
>
> Mr. Hanlon said he could not understand why five people were allowed to operate the service when the cream of the traffic was available, and only two had to carry the winter burden. All should share the winter services.
>
> He had no doubt that an adequate and fair service could be operated, and in June or July he would call a public inquiry for the service to be varied. As the winter service was scheduled to end on April 2, any immediate change might cause inconvenience.

The service started in Keswick at Moot Hall in the Market Square and not at the bus station. When returning from Seatoller, as there was no immediate place near to Moot Hall to turn around, the vehicles proceeded past and ran down towards the bus station for turning/layovers, as seen on the next page.

Weightman's Commer in 1958 back in from Seatoller and proceeding past Moot Hall to turn around.

In summer 1958 Weightman sold out to the Lake Hotel coach operation in Keswick. It has been speculated that they only wanted Weightman's excursion licence and not the stage service. Lake Hotel Coaches had been formed in 1909 to operate horse-drawn coaches and was by 1952 owned by a Mr. J.S. Wilson who then had one OB/Duple and three Bedford SBG/Yeates coaches.

The earlier mentioned February 1958 Traffic Commissioners meeting may have forced the sale by Weightman of their share of the route to Cumberland Motor Services in September 1958 and could also have finalised the three remaining operators (Askew, Simpson and Young's) to jointly form a limited company, Keswick Borrowdale Bus Services Limited (KBBS). This was incorporated in 1959 with its registered office at Victoria Street, Keswick (where Young's were based). KBBS was now therefore, the joint operator with Cumberland.

After the September 1958 sale by Weightman's of their share of the stage route, CMS had two of the five shares of the route. Weightman, now owned by Lake Hotel coaches, carried on as a one coach operation until April 1965, when along with the associated Lake Hotel excursion and tour coach operation (now only with two coaches) they were bought jointly by Cumberland and Ribble. They shared the two operators' tours/excursions licences; no vehicles were involved in the purchases. Lake Hotel and Weightman were therefore wound up with application to do so made in August 1965.

Lake Hotel Coaches of Lake Road Coaching Station are touting for excursion work alongside the wooden coach booking office/shed. From the fleet title, some would assume this operator was occupied on inclusive tours for Keswick's Lake Hotel, but the transport business was founded in 1904 and was totally devoted to serving the general public. Parked up on Lake Road are Bedford WTB CRM999 and an OB. Further down Lake Road and just around the right corner, is Moot Hall from where the Seatoller bus started. Lake Road, behind the camera, becomes Borrowdale Road and was the route out to Seatoller in 1954.

Left: *KAO265 from 1950 is an unusual Bedford OB/Duple with its rooftop windows on the Lake Hotel stand.*

Below: *For Buttermere a popular half day excursion, Lake Hotel NRM350 Bedford SBG/Yeates. New in 1954, it stayed for five years.*

Meanwhile in *Commercial Motor* dated 13th November 1959, the Northern Traffic Commissioners allowed Keswick Borrowdale Bus Services Ltd. to operate between Keswick and Seatoller, but stated that the grant was conditional upon a timetable being agreed with Cumberland Motor Services Ltd. Mr. Simpson told the Traffic Commissioners that the previously agreed KBBS amalgamation would allow savings and that the application represented the first step in effecting proposals made by the Commissioners in 1958. He said CMS had suggested that during the winter each should work the route in alternate three-monthly periods, instead of alternate weeks. Mr. Simpson could not agree to this, because he could not keep a driver idle for three months.

However, KBBS was to last less than 10 years as its partners decided to retire before the summer 1967 season and the licence now fully passed to Cumberland in March 1967. An application to wind up KBBS was published in *The London Gazette* on 27th October 1967, this being finalised in April 1968 in the liquidator's office at 43 Station Road, Keswick. The "reign of the OB" was over.

Fleet History late 1930s to 1967

Looking back and then forward to the major changes on the route in 1967, the subsequent vehicles operated by the four independents were as follows:

W.L. Askew the 1948 OB GRM914 came in 1953 and was to be replaced by another OB (KWB334) in April 1961, this one being new in January 1948 to ET White & Sons in Calver, Derbyshire and withdrawn in May 1967.

Before GRM914, between 1932 and 1936, Askew had bought a Bedford WLB and a Commer registered RM8699 and BRM198.

Left: *The Askew Bedford OB GRM914 with a SMT body waits at Seatoller. It was new in 1948 to Mandale of Greystoke, Cumberland.*

R.W. Simpson. Their earlier seen Commer HRM108 lasted until 1956 when it was replaced by an OB GAO961, from Lake Hotel Coaches. This and earlier buses are shown below:

Right: *Simpson's Ford/Willett ARM824 was new in June 1935 and ran until December 1948 after which it was scrapped and replaced by Commer HAO108.*

Ford/Willet CAO505, with Simpson's from March 1937, was sold at some point to a Richardson in Dumfriesshire. It was last licensed there in December 1954.

Simpson's GAO861, at the rear of the Moot Hall, came in 1956 from Lake Hotel Coaches in Keswick. With a June 1947 SMT C29F body it retained the Lake Hotel livery and replaced Commer HAO108. GAO861 stayed until 1962 when JRM651 replaced it.

By the Moot Hall is Simpson's OB JRM651, used from June 1962 to March 1967. The driver often waited in the Central Hotel – the white building behind the signposts. JRM651 came from Elsey in Gosberton, Lincolnshire and had been new in March 1950 to E&L Tittington, Blencow, Cumberland.

Simpsons JRM651 was joined in June 1962 by another OB, new in 1948 to Brownrigg, Egremont, and registered HAO389. The car park attendant is on patrol, and will move the wooden barrier forward once the bus departs. An Austin Healey with deer stalker hatted passengers passes by. HAO389 was withdrawn in June 1967.

T. Weightman became Weightman's (Keswick) Ltd in 1948. The earlier seen Commer HAO950 lasted until 1956 when it seems likely their 1950 Commer Avenger/Myers and Bowman coach replaced it on the Seatoller route, or perhaps more likely a coach was hired in from Lake Hotel Coaches in Keswick. The Commer's replacement would only run for two years, as Weightman's share on the Seatoller route was bought out by Cumberland in September 1958.

Left: With a shiny radiator, an earlier Weightman's bus was ARM 554, a 1935 Bedford WTB with Duple C20F, to be withdrawn in March 1951.

HAO402 was preceded by two Commers with Waveney bodies in 1936, 1937 and also in 1939 by a Bedford WTB with Emcol body. These were registered BRM199, CAO461 and DRM330, and were withdrawn in 1950, 1951 and 1945 respectively.

HAO402 was a Commer Commando with Myers & Bowman body that was new in March 1948; its withdrawal date is not known.

Weightman's Commer HAO950 was new in July 1948 and is said to have been rebuilt from a wartime lorry chassis fitted with a Myers & Bowman body. HAO950 is in its last livery before withdrawal in October 1956.

Weightman's Commer in Seatoller in 1954.

T. Young's Borrowdale Service, Keswick. OB HRM48 from 1948 was there right until the end in 1967, and was joined from 1955 to 1962 by a 1950 Leyland PS2/Burlingham FC33F coach registered CCB291, bought from Wearden in Little Harwood, Lancashire and used on excursions.

A Bedford WTB, with Duple body CRM861, came to Young's in March 1938 and was there until 1953. What it has done to attract the attention of the man in uniform remains a mystery, but the passengers are more interested in the presence of the photographer.

HRM48 lays over off Bank Street in a part of Keswick that was demolished and is now a car park.

Young's long serving HRM48 at the Seatoller terminus looks like it only has had a wash at the front. Young was an early pioneer of route branding, the side windows having stickers for the Seatoller-Borrowdale service. They also billed themselves as Young's "Red & White" Borrowdale Bus Service in the pre-war timetables.

The liveries of the four operators were as follows:

- Askew GRM914 was white and black, but KWB334 was light and dark blue. The original livery is recorded as being cream and brown
- Weightman's HAO Commer was cream with a light blue stripe, roof, front wings, and bonnet top, earlier had been overall blue and also, overall light blue with a dark blue flash.
- Simpson's HRM Commer was a dark green with a white side stripe and engine bonnet top. GAO861 from Lake Hotel is recorded as being grey with maroon stripe and JRM651 from Elsey was pale and dark green with cream side stripe and roof. The livery of HAO389 is, however, unknown, perhaps it retained Brownrigg's colours?
- Young's OB was cream and with a maroon stripe, roof, front/rear wings, and bonnet top.

Cumberland mainly used their Leyland single deckers and although an OWB was photographed on the route it seems likely their OBs were also used, as the last two were not withdrawn until 1958. Two of the CMS Leylands photographed on the route up to 1967 are seen below.

Loading for Seatoller in 1939 Keswick is this Cumberland bus at the bus station that was to be further developed in the 1950s. Fleet number 30 was a Leyland TS2 new in 1929 with a Massey B30R body. It was rebodied by Massey in April 1939 to DP32R and fitted with a Cov-Rad radiator. Sold to the dealers Norths in March 1950, it then served with Shaws in Bolton until September 1952.

Leyland PS1 from 1949, JAO836, seen on 22nd January 1964 with its smart August 1958 Cumberland body. The Cumberland Leyland Tigers were an interesting series of buses and coaches that were transformed for stage work in varied ways and are featured in a forthcoming book, provisionally titled "Cumberland Motor Services – Leyland buses (1938 to 1953) and Millom (in 1966)".

A Journey up Borrowdale

From March 1967, Cumberland ruled 100%. Since then the Borrowdale route, (by now Cumberland route number 79), has not substantially changed, apart from slight changes in Keswick as the bus station is now used, and the route slightly changed, to avoid the subsequent pedestrianised area of the Market Place/Moot Hall. The terminus at Seatoller has also changed slightly and moved forward a few yards to give a larger off-road waiting and reversing area at the entrance to a National Trust car park. Finally, around 2006 Cumberland renumbered the route to 78.

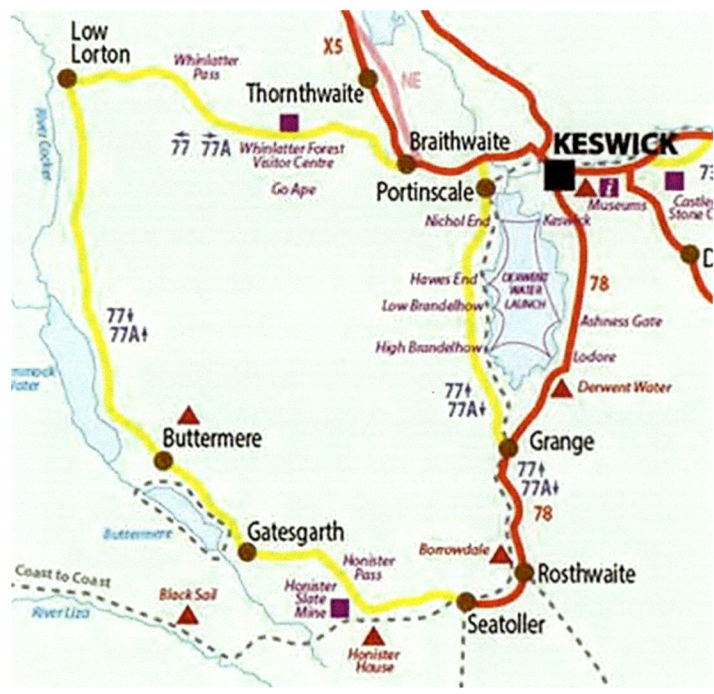

A recent map of the 78 route along with the associated circulars of route 77/77A.

The buses used by Cumberland buses since 1967 reflect their single decker fleet renewals, such as the late 1940s Leyland PS1s, Leyland Royal Tigers and Bristol SCs, MWs, RELLs and LH6Ps were all used. From the late 1970s, Leyland Nationals ruled; then came the open-top double deckers from 1996 for summer use, with Optare Solos mainly used in winter.

In the following section, covering a journey up the Borrowdale Valley, mainly Cumberland buses are seen. Cumberland were owned by the Stagecoach group from July 1987 and from mid-1988 used the Stagecoach corporate livery of white, with red, orange, and blue overlays. In April 1989 Stagecoach bought out their "next door neighbour" Ribble Motor Services and in 1990 green liveried open-top buses came to the Lake District in Ambleside. In 1991 a green painted Leyland National became "The Borrowdale bus" and in 1996, as a further reflection of the tourist nature of the route, a series of open-top double deckers were used on the route in the summer, with Optare Solos in the winter.

Coming from the Stagecoach Penrith depot, Keswick had two narrow Optare Solos for the 77 routes in 2010. Here is one on the 78, splashing its way down the valley between Rosthwaite and Grange.

A final look at two Bedford OBs with Simpson's JRM651 on layover at Keswick Bus Station, outside the double decker Cumberland depot.

Just in front of the No Exit board in the bus station, and on the opposite side from JRM651 above, is Young's HRM48 that often did its layovers in Keswick Bus Station as Young's office was nearby. The white shed, and one out of sight alongside, were joined to the single decker Cumberland depot, whose entrance was on the other side.

Tucked away in the corner near to the entry side of the bus station, LAO145 was one of five Leyland PSU1/13 with an ECW body in the LS style, apart from the curved windscreen. New in 1952 and withdrawn in 1970, it was fitted, as seen here in March 1967, with its very recently acquired fixed window windscreen.

In Keswick Bus Station yard ready for a run to Seatoller is Cumberland 166, RHN767. One of five similar buses ordered by Cumberland but diverted to United AS in 1953, they were Leyland PSU1/13 with standard ECW LS style B45F bodies. They went to CMS in 1967 for three more years' service.

In the wide-open space of Keswick Bus Station after running in from Seatoller, is Cumberland 402, XAO610 a 1959 Bristol SC4LK with ECW B35F body. With sister 403 they were the last new SCs; however, six secondhand ones came in 1963 and 1964.

Parked up in June 1975 is CMS106 a 1970 Bristol LH6P with ECW B45F body. This bus was exhibited at the 1970 Commercial Motor Show as it was the first ECW body to have the BET style wrap around windscreen. It was to be the only one at CMS, although several normal LHs came. However, the short Leyland National stopped any more LHs from being ordered.

A Cumberland rebodied JAO drops people from Borrowdale off near Moot Hall.

Leyland National 204 in 1985 has come from the bus station and is going past Moot Hall heading for the narrow Lake Road that goes off the Market Place. 204 was from a batch of fifteen delivered in 1978/79, nine of which had replaced a cancelled order for Bristol LH buses.

810 as "The Borrowdale Bus" has made it along the narrow Lake Road. Behind 810 to the left was the former, grandly named, Lake Road Coaching Station of Lake Hotel Coaches. 810 was a 1979 short Leyland National B type from Ribble and acquired by CMS in February 1986 following their takeover of the north Cumbria area of Ribble. This involved the depots at Carlisle and Penrith and three outstations at Alston, Bowness-on-Solway and Kirkoswald: along with 74 buses. All retained their Ribble fleet numbers and in 1991 810 received the "Lakeland Green" livery and "The Borrowdale Bus" badging.

231 was a 1964 Bristol MW6G with ECW body and is heading out of Keswick on 19th October 1969.

206 has come past the Lodore Hotel and runs alongside Derwentwater on its way back to Keswick.

At the Lodore Hotel B117TVU, CMS 2117 is an accidental open-top bus. New to GM Buses in February 1985 it was a Leyland Olympian with Northern Counties body. Latterly with Stagecoach Manchester, it then had a low bridge accident in the late 1990s and became, after being tidied up, an open-topper.

231 was a fixture at Keswick for many years until 1980 when it went for preservation. It has passed the Lodore Hotel (the tower in the background) and is on its way to the Borrowdale Hotel climbing the only gradient on the whole road to Seatoller.

201, with, in the background, the Borrowdale Hotel, heads up the hill for the Lodore Hotel and Keswick.

273 was a Bristol RELL new in 1968 and withdrawn in 1983 when it was replaced by a Leyland National. Bound for Seatoller, 273 has passed the Borrowdale Hotel and approaches the turn for Grange-in-Borrowdale.

Just past the turn-off for Grange-in-Borrowdale is CMS 224, a former Bristol LS6G coach with ECW body new in 1954. In a batch of three and the first Bristol single deckers for CMS, it was the only one to be rebuilt and converted to a bus when it was reseated to B45F by ECW in April 1967. In October 1970 it left normal service, two years after the other two from the batch had been withdrawn and became a driver training vehicle. Later a mobile office, it was withdrawn by 1980.

This Bristol VR was new to Southdown in 1978 and was built as a convertible open-top bus. It was with East Kent from 1991 to 1994, Ribble from 1994 to 1996 before being with Cumberland from March 1996 to December 2001. It was one of the first open-toppers on the route and was the only one to have a rear fitted cycle rack. Numbered 2076 it is possibly near to the Bowder Stone just after Grange.

Back to October 1965 with Simpson's JRM651 heading to Seatoller and near to the Bowder Stone.

Cumberland 1944 OWB 85 returning to Keswick and passing through Rosthwaite, the village below Seatoller. It had a short life with Cumberland and in 1952 went to the contractors Higgs & Hill who had their HQ in London; it stayed with them until 1956.

Opposite: *231 leaving Seatoller and two coaches in the car park. A regular for many years on the route with sister 232, both were withdrawn in 1980 and 231 is now preserved. An observer noted the contrast with the former OBs: "The contrast between the well-kept OBs and the intrusion of the new-fangled MW was quite something. Although the legal capacity of the OBs was considerably less than the MW, the practical capacity of the OB was defined as all those that wanted to go! The OBs always managed to keep the customer happy".*

Forward to 2013 and one of the newer generation of open-toppers waits at Seatoller. The four buses required in the summer are garaged in Penrith, a 37-mile round trip every day. Penrith also has two open-toppers for a route to Ullswater. Kendal has eight for the Windermere "Lakes Connection" service.

Stagecoach 17217 has turned at Seatoller and is now returning to Keswick. The bus is a Dennis Trident with Alexander body that was new to Stagecoach East London in 2000 with an H71D body and is now PO70F. It came north in 2011 and is one of four open-top double decker buses used in the peak summer period.